READING

RECOVERY

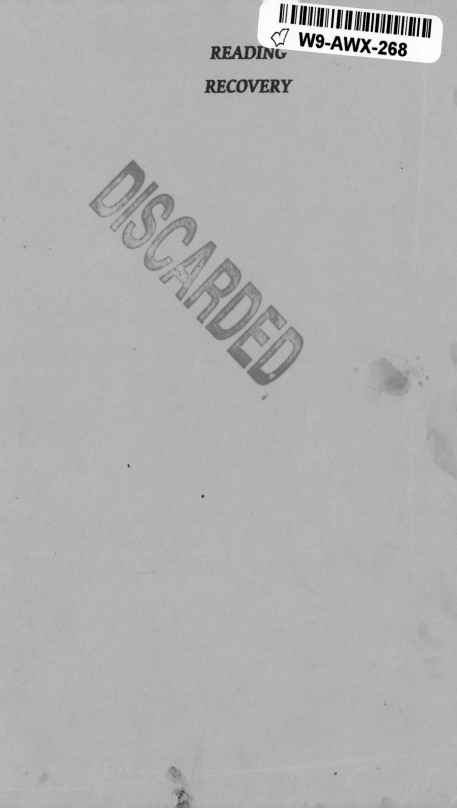

RED FOX
and his
CANOE

An I CAN READ Book®

RED FOX
and his
CANOE

by
NATHANIEL BENCHLEY
PICTURES BY ARNOLD LOBEL

HARPER & ROW, PUBLISHERS

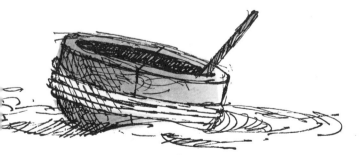

I Can Read Book is a registered trademark of
Harper & Row, Publishers, Inc.

RED FOX AND HIS CANOE
Text copyright © 1964 by Nathaniel Benchley
Pictures copyright © 1964 by Arnold Lobel
Printed in the United States of America.

Library of Congress catalog card number: 64-16650
ISBN 0-06-020476-1 (lib. bdg.)

Like all Indian boys,

Red Fox had a canoe

to go fishing in.

But he wanted a bigger one.

So he went to his father
and said,

"I need a new canoe.

Will you make me a bigger one?"

"Sure," said his father.

"How big a one do you want?"

9

I want the biggest canoe

in the whole world," said Red Fox.

"Bigger than any other there is."

"That may not be a good idea,"

said his father.

"But let's go to the woods

and see."

So they went
to the woods,
where his father
looked at trees
for a canoe.
Each time his father
saw a tree,
Red Fox saw
a bigger one.

Finally his father cut down

a tree and made a fire in it.

"This is too big for you.

But never mind. You'll grow," he said.

14

Red Fox, who was helping scrape
the burned wood out of the tree, said,
"No canoe is too big for me.
The bigger, the better, I say."

When all the burned wood
was scraped out, his father said,
"All right, here's your canoe.
Can you lift it?"
"Sure," said Red Fox.
"Easily."

So they put it in the water,

and Red Fox paddled off.

"Oh, boy!" he said.

"Now watch me catch

a million fish!"

19

He fished for a long time

and was nearing the half million mark

when he heard some strange noises.

SPLASH! CRUNCH! SPLAT!

So he went to look . . .

and there was a bear in the water

trying to catch fish.

When Red Fox got a little closer,

the bear saw him

and saw all his fish.

"Hey!" said the bear.

"That's just what I've been
looking for!"

"Hey, cut that out!" said Red Fox.

"Those fish are mine!"

"Not now, they're not,"

said the bear.

And he ate them all.

"Can I go now?" Red Fox asked

when the bear was through.

"Sure," said the bear.

"And I'm coming too.

This is the best way to fish.

Now get going!"

So Red Fox got going.

After a while

the bear saw a friend.

"Look here!" he said.

"Come on out

and join the party!"

"Can Al come, too?"

said the friend.

"Sure," said the bear.

"It's a big canoe.

Bring Al along, too."

33

So Al came along, too.

And all three bears caught fish

while Red Fox paddled.

How could he get rid of the bears?

Then Red Fox thought of a trick

to get rid of the bears.

"Hey, look here!" he said.

"Look in the water!"

All the bears

turned and looked,

and the canoe tipped

way over.

But before Red Fox

could tip it all the way,

two otters came aboard.

"Thank you," said one otter.

"We were getting

tired of the water."

"It's lucky this is a big canoe,"

said the other otter.

"We can do our fishing

from here."

"Go over that way.

There are more fish there."

As they passed underneath

the limb of a tree

a raccoon jumped into the canoe.

"Excuse me," he said.

"I want to wash a piece of meat."

Then the bears began to get sleepy.

"You," said one of them to Red Fox.

"Move over. I want to take a nap."

"I can't," said Red Fox.

"I have no place to move."

"Then get out of the boat,"

said the bear.

"It's all the same to me."

"I will not!" said Red Fox.

"This is *my* canoe! *You* get out!"

"It's a big canoe," said the bear.

"There's room for all."

And he went to sleep.

Red Fox was pushed out of the
canoe, onto the front part.

"At least *you* might leave,"
he said to the otters.

"This *is* my canoe, you know."

"We're sleepy, too," said the otters.

44

And they climbed up on the bears

and went to sleep.

"How about you?"

Red Fox said to the raccoon.

"Will you let me get back in my canoe?"

Before the raccoon could answer,

a moose came by.

"This looks like fun," he said.

"May I come in, too?"

"Come *in?*" said Red Fox.

"Are you *crazy?*"

But the moose put one foot

in the canoe

and there was a loud C R A C K !

And no more canoe.

"Did I do something wrong?"

asked the moose.

"Oh, no," said one of the bears.

"You just broke our canoe, that's all."

"Sorry," said the moose.

"It looked like a public canoe

to me."

And he went away.

All that was left were the front

and back ends of the canoe.

So Red Fox put them together
and tied them tightly
with vines and branches
and birch bark.

The new canoe was, if anything,
a little smaller than his first one.
But it floated.

And it got him home.

And everybody cheered.

Except his father, who didn't believe

a word of it.

E
BEN

Benchley, Nathaniel.

7261

Red Fox and his
canoe.

**DANIEL ST. THOMAS JENIFER
ELEMENTARY SCHOOL**